Moving to Britain from Lithuania

By Deborah Chancellor
Photography by Chris Fairclough

FRANKLIN WATTS
LONDON•SYDNEY

First published in 2008 by Franklin Watts

Franklin Watts,
338 Euston Road,
London, NW1 3BH

Franklin Watts Australia,
Level 17/207 Kent Street,
Sydney, NSW 2000

Series editor: Sarah Peutrill
Art director: Jonathan Hair
Design: Rita Storey
Photographs: Chris Fairclough (unless otherwise stated)

The Author and Photographer would like to thank the following for their
help in the preparation of this book: Andra, Guste and Juste and
the staff and pupils at the Mulberry Primary School, Tottenham.

Picture credits: Family's personal photographs: cover (inset), 13, 14, 25, 27t,
27tr. bluliq/Shutterstock:10b. Marc C. Johnson/Shutterstock: 11t.
ronfromyork/Shutterstock:15tr. selensergen/istockphoto: 29.
Vaida/Shutterstock: 11b, 12b. Every attempt has been made to clear
copyright. Should there be any inadvertent omission please apply to the
publisher for rectification.

Dewey number: 304.8'41'0469

ISBN: 978 0 7496 7859 3

Printed in China

Franklin Watts is a division of Hachette Children's Books,
an Hachette Livre UK company.

Contents

All about me   6

Meet my family   8

About Lithuania   10

My life in Lithuania   12

Moving to Britain   14

Our home   16

Going to school   18

My school day   20

My free time   22

Keeping traditions   24

My future   26

Glossary   28

Lithuania fact file   29

Index and Further information   30

Words in **bold** are in the glossary on page 28.

All about me

My name is Guste, which sounds like 'Goustay' when you say it out loud. I am eight years old and I live in Tottenham, in north London. I love art and, in my free time, I am always drawing pictures.

I like designing new fashions. I go to an art club after school.

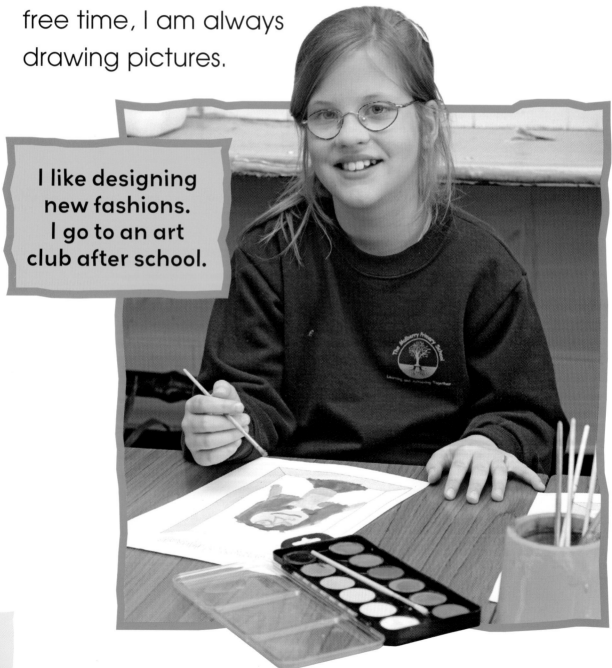

At school I speak English with my friends. At home I speak Lithuanian with my family.

My family comes from Lithuania. I learned to speak **Lithuanian** when I was little. I started speaking English when I moved to Britain, two and a half years ago.

Meeting people

Try talking in Lithuanian!

What is your name?
Koks tavo vardas?

My name is ...
Mano vardas ...

Hello
Labas

Goodbye
Viso gero

Look out for more Lithuanian words in this book!

Meet my family

I live with my mum, dad and sister. My sister is my twin. She is called Juste, and is seven minutes older than me. Some people can't tell us apart!

Family words

Mum	*Mama*
Father	*Tetis*
Grandma	*Senele*
Grandpa	*Senelis*

This is us with our mum. I'm the one wearing glasses!

Most of the time my sister and I get on very well. We like to play **basketball** together.

Basketball is the most popular sport in Lithuania. It is more popular than football.

Some of my family still live in Lithuania. My grandparents live in a city called Kaunas. Juste and I were born in Kaunas, and we spent a lot of time with our grandparents when we were small. Now we go back to Kaunas every summer, to stay with them.

I miss my grandparents, but I can talk to them on the phone.

About Lithuania

Lithuania is not a big country, but you can find it on a globe if you look carefully.

Lithuania has **borders** with four other countries.

Lithuania is a country in Eastern **Europe**. It takes about three hours to fly from London to Vilnius, the **capital** of Lithuania. Lithuania has a **population** of 3.5 million people.

Lithuania

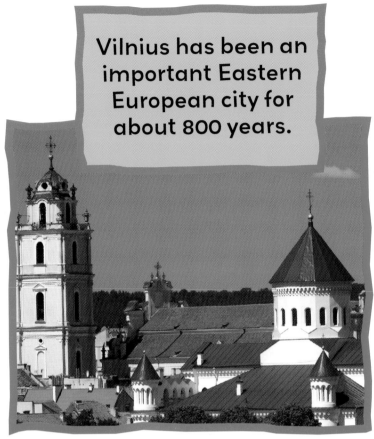

Vilnius has been an important Eastern European city for about 800 years.

Lithuania has a **coast** on the Baltic Sea. Inland, there are lots of farms, and many pine forests and pretty lakes. The country is famous for its **jazz** music.

Lithuania's coastline is about 100 km long. It is lined with sand dunes and forests.

My life in Lithuania

LITHUANIA

Kaunas

VILNIUS

Kaunas is in west Lithuania, about 90 km from Vilnius.

My sister and I lived in the city of Kaunas before we moved to London. We lived in a tiny apartment with our mum and dad. Our grandparents lived in a big house with a garden. They had two dogs, so we always liked visiting them.

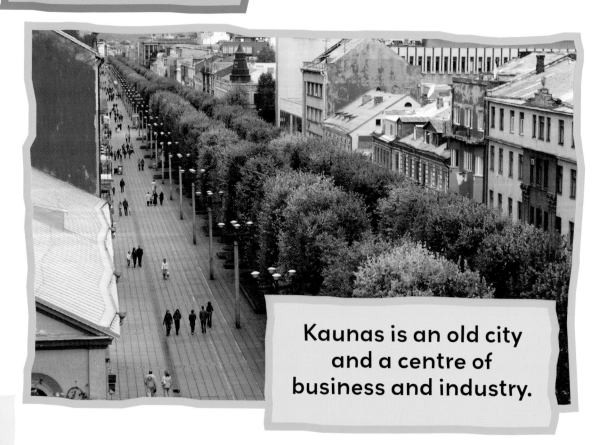

Kaunas is an old city and a centre of business and industry.

When Juste and I were three years old, we started going to a **nursery** in Kaunas. We spent all day at this nursery, and had all our meals there. We were supposed to have a nap in the afternoon, but sometimes we just pretended to sleep!

This is Juste and me with our Grandpa, not long before we started at nursery. I am sitting next to Grandpa.

Moving to Britain

When my sister and I were three years old, Mum and Dad moved to Britain to find work. They were very sad, because they had to leave us with our grandparents. They missed us a lot.

Our grandparents looked after us very well when Mum and Dad went to live in London.

Juste and I moved to Britain when we were six. We flew here on a plane with our grandpa.

Juste, Guste's twin sister says:

"I had never been on a plane before I came to Britain. I was nervous about getting on the plane, and thought it might fall out of the sky!"

We came to live with Mum and Dad in Tottenham in north London. We were so excited to be with our parents again!

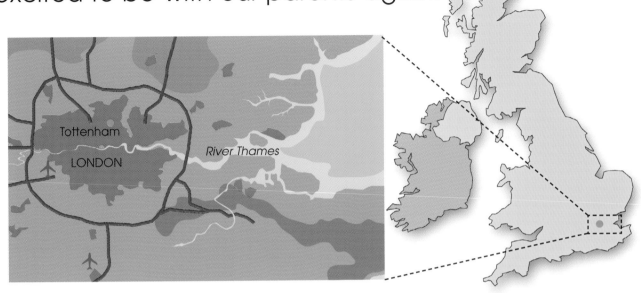

At first, Tottenham seemed huge and very crowded.

There are so many people in London, from many countries. Kaunas is a much smaller city.

Our home

Juste and I share a bedroom. We like playing games on our Playstation.

Our home in Tottenham is bigger than our old home in Kaunas. There is more space to run around and play hide and seek, and we have a garden too.

Every day, my dad leaves home early to go to work. He is a **shopfitter** in London. My mum works as a cleaner near our home. This means she can take Juste and me to school in the morning, and pick us up in the afternoon.

We have a nice park near our home. Sometimes we go there after school.

Going to school

In Lithuania, children don't start school until they are six years old. When my sister and I lived in Lithuania, we were not old enough to go to school. Now we live in Tottenham, we go to a school near our home called Mulberry Primary.

We started at Mulberry Primary in Year 1. We are now in Year 3.

One of our first teachers here was Miss Irvine. She did some fun activities with us to help us learn the English **language.** We had two special lessons with her every week. At first we only knew a few words, but this soon changed!

My school day

My best friend is called Paula. Her family also comes from Lithuania.

In Lithuania, children often have the same teacher for their whole time at primary school. In Britain, we have a different teacher every year. My teacher this year is called Mr Kelly.

Mr Kelly, Guste's teacher says:

"Guste and Juste are wonderful to teach. They are keen to learn, work very hard and are great **role models** for the whole class."

In Lithuanian schools, children start at 8am and finish at about 2pm. In Britain, we start and finish later than this. We take packed lunches to school.

Juste and I like sitting with our friends in the dining hall. It is a good chance to chat and laugh together.

After lunch, we have fun playing outside in the playground.

My free time

When I play with Guste, we speak and argue in Lithuanian. This is our first language, and the one we know best.

At the weekend, I like to go out with my family. Sometimes Mum and Dad take Juste and me to play at our local park. We like going on the climbing frame there.

I enjoy reading at home. My mum likes me to practise reading in Lithuanian, as well as in English. We have lots of Lithuanian books at home.

I read a lot of stories, but I also like reading about real things, such as Ancient Egypt.

Keeping traditions

In Lithuania, we have some fun **traditions**. At Easter, a mysterious old lady called the 'Easter Granny' leaves children eggs in a basket. Juste and I write to Granny at Easter, and she sends us cards and presents if we have been good.

Mum checks that I have written Granny a good letter. If not, I have to write it again.

This is a photo of Juste and me on our 3rd birthday when we were in Lithuania.

Another special time is 'Children's Day', on 1st June. Children are given treats on this day.

We also like to celebrate birthdays! Juste and I have had two birthdays in Britain. We always share a cake and blow out the candles to make a wish.

Special greetings

Here are some Lithuanian greetings for special days of the year.

Happy Birthday
Su gimtadieniu

Happy Easter
Sveiki sulauke Sv velyku

Merry Christmas
Linksmu Kaledu

My future

When I grow up, I think I would like to be a **journalist**, because I like finding out about things. My sister Juste would like to write books. She is always writing stories on our computer at home.

We both work hard on our homework. Juste and I are in top groups now, and our parents are very proud of us.

I have lived in Britain for over two years. I am used to it now, and I do not miss Lithuania as much as I did at first. But Lithuania is the country where I was born, and maybe I will live there again one day.

We like looking at old photos, to remind us of our time in Lithuania.

Glossary

basketball
A team game in which players try to throw a ball through a high hoop to score points.

borders
Lines, or boundaries, that separate two countries.

capital
The most important city in a country.

coast
The seashore, and the land that is near the sea.

Europe
One of the seven continents – large areas of land – of the world.

jazz
A kind of modern music with a strong rhythm.

journalist
Somebody who writes for newspapers, magazines or television news.

language
The words you speak or write to communicate with other people. Different languages are spoken in different countries.

Lithuanian
Somebody who comes from Lithuania. This is also the name for the language that is spoken in Lithuania.

nursery
A place that cares for children who are too young to go to school.

population
The number of people that live in a place.

role model
Somebody who is a good example to other people.

shopfitter
A craftsperson who builds and decorates the insides of shops.

tradition
A belief, custom or habit that has not changed for a very long time.

translate
To change something from one language to another, so people can understand.

Lithuania fact file

• About 3.5 million people live in Lithuania today. Almost 3 million people from Lithuania now live in other countries around the world.

• Over 7 million people live in London. That is twice the number of people that live in the whole of Lithuania.

• London, Britain's capital city, is 1,730 km away from Vilnius, the capital city of Lithuania.

• Lithuanian is one of the oldest languages in the world that is still spoken by people today.

• In Lithuania, most people follow the Roman Catholic faith. Some people are Protestant, Russian Orthodox, Jewish and Muslim.

• In Lithuania, people use a currency called the litas. One hundred centas make up one litas – like in the British currency, which has one hundred pennies in a pound.

• In Lithuania, primary and secondary schools are often found together in the same big building. Children stay at primary school for four years.

Lithuanian flag

Index

birthdays 25

Children's Day 25

Easter Granny 24
English, learning 7, 19, 23

friends 7, 13, 20, 21, 23

jazz 11, 28

Kaunas 9, 12, 13, 15, 16

Lithuania 7, 9, 10–11, 18, 20, 21, 24, 27, 29
capital 10, 28, 29
landscape 11
map 10, 12
population 10
Lithuanian language 7, 8, 25, 29

school 7, 17, 18–21, 26, 29
sport 9

Tottenham 6, 15, 16, 18

Further information

www.lithuaniatourism.co.uk
http://neris.mii.lt
These websites give some general information about Lithuania.

www.kaunas.lt/
This website gives information about the city of Kaunas, where Guste and her family come from.

www.kaunasjazz.lt
This website gives information about the Kaunas Jazz Festival.

Note to parents and teachers: Please note that these websites are **not** specifically for children and we strongly advise that Internet access is supervised by a responsible adult.